When is My Time?

WHEN IS MY TIME?

TAMARA ELCAN BALDWIN

I dedicate this book to my grandparents.
Thank you for your love, patience, support,
encouragement, words of wisdom,
and most importantly, your prayers.
I miss you all, but I know you are
always with me in spirit.
I pray that I have made you proud!

Love you,

Tamara

CONTENTS

FOREWORD
BY BISHOP GREGORY M. FULLER

One of the greatest honors afforded to any pastor is to serve as a spiritual father or mother for one of God's called and chosen servants. I have been afforded this great honor, serving as the spiritual father for the Reverend Tamara Baldwin.

Over the years, Reverend Baldwin has proven herself to be a dedicated, loving, faithful servant of God and student of God's Word. Her love for people and their spiritual and emotional growth is infectious. She generally cares for people. Her love and care for others is evidence of her sincere desire to see people grow to spiritual maturity so they might live out their purpose. Her book, *When is My Time?* is simply a manifestation of her passion for the growth of others.

When is My Time? answers the questions of "why is it taking so long for me to get my blessing?" "my husband?" "my wife?" "my breakthrough?" "my deliverance?" In this book, Reverend Baldwin not only gives encouragement to persons who are waiting for "their time," but she also provides necessary encouragement and instruction as to what one should be doing while they are waiting on "their time."

Some would think this to be a book for singles waiting on a spouse but that would not be a correct assessment of this work. This is a book for singles, couples, and anyone else who is waiting on anything from God. This is a book for all.

As Reverend Baldwin points out, it is not just about waiting but what you do while you are waiting. King David in the last verse of Psalm 27 encourages us to "wait on the Lord; be of good courage, and he shall strengthen your heart, wait I say upon the Lord" (Psalm 27:14)! The Hebrew word used here for "wait" does not mean to sit and do nothing. The word actually means to bind together, expect, look for, and patiently tarry in anticipation of. Thus, while we are waiting we should bind ourselves to the purpose and plans of God, patiently waiting or the fulfillment of God's promises. Reverend Baldwin gives us practical, theological advice and encouragement as to what we should be doing while we are waiting on "our time."

As previously stated, this is a book for all. For all should be waiting, expecting, anticipating greater and much more from a God who can do "exceedingly above all that we can ask or think . . ." (Ephesians 3:20).

I give God all praise for Reverend Tamara Baldwin and her, "breaking out of her comfort zone" to allow God to use her to encourage and be a blessing to others. To Reverend Baldwin I say, "this is just the beginning" and "the best is yet to come."

—**BISHOP, GREGORY M. FULLER,**
Doctor of Ministry
Pastor, Macedonia Church of Augusta, (USA)
Presiding Prelate, Abba's Army Apostolic Alliance

INTRODUCTION

I looked over my life and everything "I" was doing—serving God, keeping myself for my future husband, preaching the gospel on Sundays and ministering to others outside of the church walls. I still had not received the blessings God had revealed and promised me. It has been over 20 years since I've gotten divorced. To tell the truth, I would have never thought I would be single for this long, and not even have a steady long-term relationship.

Not to boast, but I'm not an unattractive woman, I have a good job, I consider myself pretty intelligent, and I have a great credit score, and most of all I love the Lord. So why am I still single? Why are the things God has revealed to me not come to pass?

Maybe you have never felt the "Why am I in this situation, God?" I see *everyone* (when you get into your feelings it feels and looks like everyone) around me is getting married. Everyone else is getting promoted Everyone else is getting healed. Everyone else is being blessed. Don't get me wrong, I'm happy for them, I celebrate them, and I celebrate what God is doing for them, but *when is my time?*

God put in my spirit that there were a few things He wanted me to do in this season of singleness. One, He wanted me to write a book about waiting for your time. Sometimes it feels like you're on a mountain or in a valley all alone and you are the only one going through what you're going through. I am not the only one waiting for a blessing. I am not the only one waiting for a breakthrough. I am not the only one WAITING. However, just as God put into my spirit to write this book, there are things God is waiting for every one of us to do. Truthfully, as God spoke to me to write a book, *I thought* it should be geared toward singles, but God revealed that each topic and each focus is not only for singles. It is for everyone who is waiting.

When is My Time? is not only for and about singles. It is not about getting married. *When is My Time?* is about all the prayers that have gone forth, the promises received from God, and the process (time) you go through waiting on those promises to come to fruition. Everyone and I mean EVERYONE goes through a "When is my time?" season. Seasons may last a week, month, year, or even decades. However, no matter how long your season may be, know if God said it, it shall come to pass. Isaiah 55:11 says His Word will not return to Him void. Believe it and you shall receive it.

It doesn't matter if you're single or married, male or female. Your economical situation doesn't matter neither does your geographical location. God's Word is true. We see others being blessed in areas where we want to receive favor and we wonder, *When is my time?* Prayerfully this book will provide a sense of hope, a sense of comfort, a sense of peace, a sense of encouragement, and a sense of direction. Whether you are waiting on marriage, a child, becoming debt-free, receiving healing, a fruitful business, a new home, or a promotion, know you are not alone in the *When is My Time?* season.

CHAPTER ONE

Planted With a Purpose

*He also spoke this parable: A certain man had a fig tree
planted in his vineyard, and he came seeking fruit on
it and found none. Then he said to the keeper of his
vineyard, 'Look, for three years I have come seeking fruit
on this fig tree and find none. Cut it down; why does it
use up the ground?' But he answered and said to him,
'Sir, let it alone this year also, until I dig around it and
fertilize it. And if it bears fruit, well. But if not, after that
you can cut it down.'*

—Luke 13:6-9

Iremember when I was a little girl going outside
to the backyard and planting seeds with my
grandfather. I wondered how something so small
was capable of producing something much larger
and in many cases, bringing forth not just one item,
but multiple ones from only one planted seed. My

grandfather and I would plant tomatoes, cucumbers, and cabbage seeds. And when we planted tomatoes, cucumbers, and cabbage seeds, we expected tomatoes, cucumbers, and cabbage to grow.

In this parable, Jesus is talking about us and God. Just like my grandfather and I planted seeds in the garden and expected something to grow, God has "planted" us here (His seed) on earth—and he expects us to produce good fruit. Each of us are called to a purpose and that purpose is the will of God. Is your will, the will of God? Jesus asked in Luke 22: 42, "Father, if it is your will, take this cup away from Me, nevertheless not My will, but Yours be done." (NKJV Even Jesus recognized that His will may not be God's will and asked for God's will to be done. Sometimes God's will may seem strange, unusual, or even abnormal. But His will is better than any desire, dream, or purpose, we may have.

In Luke 13:6, we see "A certain man had a fig tree in his vineyard." The first question that comes to my mind is, "What is a fig tree doing in a vineyard?" A vineyard is where you grow grapes, not figs.

My friends tell me that sometimes I'm too analytical, but that's the engineer in me! But why was this fig tree planted in a vineyard? Many people wonder *Why am I at this particular job? Why am I in this current position?* or *Why am I in this current relationship?*

They say things like, "I shouldn't be here with my current experience, my current education, my current training, or my current aspirations."

Back then, when I planted seeds along with my grandfather, it was acceptable for us to plant similar plants together. But someone with a little experience in gardening might point out to me that different plants, different fruit or vegetables, and different flowers have different demands on the soil. Some need to be watered daily. Others, like cactus might like dry heat. Still others need plenty of sun light, while a few need to be planted in shaded areas. Then there are those that may be self-sufficient and adaptable no matter where you plant them. Like the plants, we all have different needs and different demands. Everyone is different, but everyone is planted with a purpose. And it's not just *a* purpose, it is a specific purpose. We may be currently planted with pumpkin seeds, but God has called us to be watermelons. Don't try to figure out why you are with the pumpkins, continue to grow and be the best watermelon God has called you to be.

When you first plant a seed or a new tree, you won't get a bloom or fruit from it right away. Think about when you were first born. There's a difference in who you were then and who you are today, correct? Not only have you grown in stature, you have grown in knowledge, you have grown in wisdom, and prayerfully, you have grown in maturity. Year after year, you have become bigger and bigger. Now some people may have grown faster in stature and some may have grown faster in knowledge but there's nothing wrong with the speed in which you grew.

Let's look at the tree in the parable. For three consecutive years, this man came to look for fruit but found none. Why didn't this particular tree show any signs of fruit within three years? After three years you would expect to see some signs of fruit. Wouldn't you?

God expects fruit from the tree, as most people expect a new job, a house, a car, a spouse, health, prosperity, and good grades. But, how many times do we want to walk away or give up on what God has planted only because it's not what we want or it is not happening in *our* timing?

Notice that the owner of the vineyard (God) didn't need a lot of persuading from the vine-dresser (Jesus). When the vine-dresser said, "Give it one more year," He didn't say, "No, it's finished. That's enough." He said, "Fine. I will give it one more year."

Remember, a fig tree represents God's blessing, and like many plants that need moisture and nutrients from the soil to sustain its growth, we need spiritual nutrients. We must be fed God's Word and lean on His guidance.

Every year the tree remained barren, it is assumed to be a loss to the owner. He could have used this same ground to plant a productive tree. Every year we wonder *when is our time coming? When will I get my blessing? When will I live a prosperous life?* The real question is, "What is the fig tree providing to the other vines and fruit trees in the vineyard?" Who are you blessing in this season? Let's look at it this way. This fig tree may not have had figs on it, however it was a large beautiful tree with many leaves on it, and it provided shade to others.

Was this fig tree providing nutrients to the other trees in the vineyard? Was the tree being more developed and getting stronger at the foundation? Were the complex roots becoming stronger to handle the storm that other trees might not be able to handle? Was a famine coming and this tree would provide food when the others wouldn't? What you have and where you are, aren't for you. You are planted with a purpose.

The other thing to notice in this parable was that the fig tree was not *just* given another year. God doesn't only give another chance, He does something positive. During that time, the vine-dresser loosened the soil around the tree so that moisture could get to the roots and he put fertilizer in the ground. Basically, Jesus is doing something special for this fig tree. He is making sure the tree gets extra nutrients. He is giving extra attention, extra love, and an extra portion of grace. While you're in this season, look at the current favor over your life. Look at the mercy God has granted you.

Mark 11:13 states, "And seeing from afar a fig tree having leaves, He went to see if perhaps He would find something on it. When He came to it, He found nothing but leaves, for it was not the season for figs."

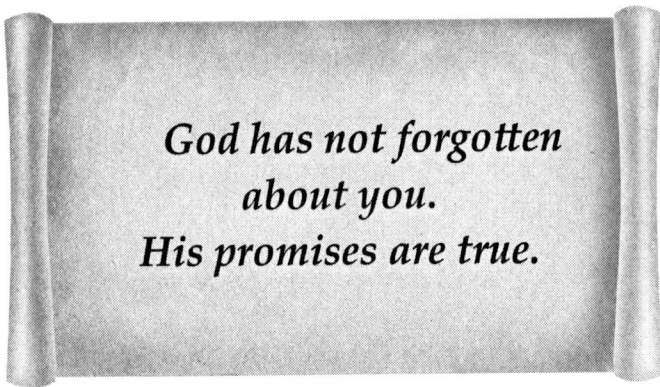

> **God has not forgotten about you. His promises are true.**

It is assumed the fig tree in the parable was supposed to bear fruit. It had been planted for a specific purpose. But "in this season" it did not bear fruit. Although the tree is given another chance to produce fruit within one more year, it is assumed that a fruit tree which has failed to bring forth fruit for three years is not going to produce fruit. To be realistic, most people would think it's impossible.

The seed of God is planted in us and it grows more and more each day but we must allow Him to grow, and grow in His timing. God's timing is not our timing. No, we might not see it right away, but we are growing each day. Can you see a plant grow? Do plants stop growing when you turn away or go to sleep or close your eyes?

Most people would feel that this fig tree would never bear fruit unless a miracle happened. There must be a transformation in the fruit tree. There must be a transformation in you. The question is, "What is its purpose?" What's your purpose? Are you trying to produce apples and God has called you to produce grapes? You might not be where you want to be and maybe you're looking for God to make a change. Remember, you're planted with a purpose and God is using you right where you are now.

Proverbs 27:18 says, "Whoever keeps the fig tree will eat its fruit; So he who waits on his master will be honored."

You're planted with a purpose. Your time is coming. Those things that you prayed and fasted for, those things that have been promised to you, are still in the atmosphere. My encouragement to you is keep walking worthy of the Lord, be fruitful in every good work and know you are planted with a purpose. Life isn't about finding another person or even finding yourself. Life is about discovering and being who God created you to be.

~NOTES~

~NOTES~

CHAPTER TWO

Please! Please! Please!

Walk worthy of the Lord pleasing Him, being fruitful in every good work and increasing in the knowledge of God.
Colossians 1:10

Pleasing God. Let's think about it. Are our actions pleasing God? Is what we're saying pleasing to God? Let's get a little deeper ... are our thoughts pleasing God? You know He knows even our thoughts. Pleasing God requires us to live in a manner that some of our so-called friends may walk away from us. Pleasing God requires us to change our attitude. Pleasing God will require us to think before we speak. Pleasing God may require us to change the places we go. Pleasing God may require us to change what we watch on TV. Pleasing God requires us to pray. Pleasing God requires us to spend more time with Him. Pleasing God will take growth and commitment!

We are also called to be fruitful in every good work. To be fruitful means our works must multiply. In order for our works to multiply we must do something. We can't multiply nothing because zero times zero is zero. So how can we be fruitful in good works if there aren't any works? Don't say you're too young, or too old or not smart enough or don't have enough resources. Like I stated in the previous chapter, God has created everyone with a purpose and a plan. Every one of us has "a good work" inside of us and by doing this good work we please Him. Everyone can help someone, everyone can be kind, and everyone can show love. Everyone "can" but not everyone does.

Sis. Bass, a mother at my church, always says, "Love is as love does." That means, you say you love me but what are you doing? What do your actions say? What are you demonstrating? But even the nicest, most loving person sometimes get some rotten fruit into their basket. Rotten fruit can come in many forms: jealousy, hatred, meanness, hurtfulness, and anger. We can't let those things that are not of God enter into our lives and our hearts and take over. God expects our lives to show love, joy, peace, kindness, goodness, faithfulness, gentleness, and self-control. We should be friendly and caring for others. Not only are we to please God and bear good fruit we're to increase in the knowledge of God.

INCREASE IN THE KNOWLEDGE OF GOD

Most of us went to school for some period of time. Why did we go to school or why do we send our children to school? School teaches us math, history, other subjects, and even social skills. Here in America, according to the law, one must go to school up until a certain age. An education teaches us how to survive in the world. We don't know what we don't know; therefore someone else must teach us. Don't you think learning about God, who He is, and His purpose and plan for our life is as important as learning 2+2?

We don't go to school for only one or two days, we go for years because we're not going to get it all in one day. Don't be discouraged or upset if you don't presently know or understand God's purpose for your life. Don't get discouraged if sometimes your actions and thoughts aren't pleasing to God. It takes having a long-term, intimate relationship with God. It takes spending time with Him on a daily basis to learn and understand how to please Him. And even then, the struggle is real, because the enemy will come and attack.

Like in school, the teacher may give you homework and you must study. You study because there will be a test (and you want to pass). Going to school is not much different than going to church and Bible study. The church prepares you for life and all the tests you will experience. Each experience, test, trial, and tribulation builds you up and grows you for where God is trying to take you.

Blessed is the man who endures temptation; for when he has been approved, he will receive the crown of life which the Lord has promised to those who love Him (**James 1:12**).

We have a book to read, a study guide that gives us our instructions. It's the Bible. Probably no one in the world can get everything they need from the Bible overnight. Truthfully, unless you are a speed-reader and a genius you won't even remember half of what you read in one night.

When I was in high school, prior to taking a test I would take my book and put it under my pillow and pray for osmosis the night before … it didn't work then and it won't work now. We must take the time and study God's Word because there will be a test. Passing the test will please God. How much you know will determine how well you do on the test and how many times you'll have to go through the test. Therefore we must continue to increase our knowledge and seek understanding.

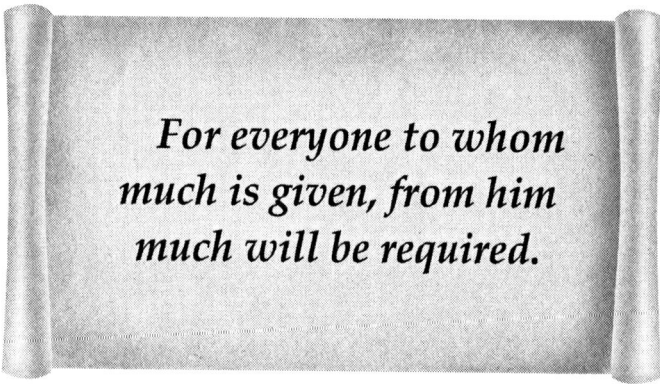

> *For everyone to whom much is given, from him much will be required.*

When taking the test, you won't be able to look at your neighbor's paper. You won't be able to write the answers on your shoe, and although the Word of God is available, you won't be able to have an open book test, and you won't be able to phone a friend. You will need to know what thus says the Lord to get through the test, to get through the storm. You must put in some study time, and do some research.

I know I want *much* therefore God requires much from me. What have you asked God for? What are you expecting from God? Have you ever wondered if God is preparing you for something GREAT? Is your purpose one that requires more to prepare for than others? Are you pleasing God in your thoughts and in your actions?

PLEASE! PLEASE! PLEASE!

~NOTES~

_____

_____

_____

_____

_____

_____

_____

_____

_____

_____

_____

_____

_____

_____

_____

_____

_____

~NOTES~

CHAPTER THREE

Let it Go!

When He had called the people to Himself, with His disciples also, He said to them, 'Whoever desires to come after Me, let him deny himself, and take up his cross, and follow Me. For whoever desires to save his life will lose it, but whoever loses his life for My sake and the gospel's will save it. For what will it profit a man if he gains the whole world, and loses his own soul?'

Mark 8:34-36

Let it go. That's an action statement that means you must do something. It's not for God to do, but for YOU to do. When Jesus spoke of losing our lives to gain our souls, He meant that we need to let go of greed, let go of selfishness, let go of covetousness, let go of jealousy. He meant that we need to look beyond our own self-interest to care for others as much as we care for ourselves.

What are you holding on to that won't let you move to where God is calling you? What are you holding on to that is keeping you from your blessing? What are you holding on to that won't allow you to have a breakthrough? For most of us it's our past.

THE PAST

Many of us allow our history to keep us from our destiny. Maybe you've had a friendship that went bad and you just can't let it go. Maybe something happened in your family 15 years ago but it feels like yesterday and you dread attending every family reunion because of the memories. Maybe someone hurt you and you keep reliving that experience over and over. Holding on to the anger, resentment, and bitterness will hurt you more than the person you are angry with.

You must put away all bitterness, anger, wrath, quarreling, and slanderous talk—indeed all malice. Instead, be kind to one another, compassionate, forgiving one another, just as God in Christ also forgave you (**Ephesians 4:31-32**).

Letting go is one of the hardest things to do because it's a mind and heart thing. But we must trust that God has something bigger and better. Letting go of a relationship, past failures, worry, hurt, fear, mistakes, sin, guilt, slander, anger, and regrets is not as easy as it sounds. It's not like you're holding a pen or pencil and someone says "let it go" and you drop it. Letting go is easier when we give it to God and realize He is in control. Don't trust in those thoughts that might come to your head, those things that may trouble your heart. Trust in the Lord. Allow Him to be in control. Don't allow your thoughts to control you.

Realize that God has allowed and used these things and those people in our life not to hurt us, not to destroy us, not to kill us, not to bury us ... but to build us, stretch us, and grow us. We must trust the plan God has for us.

> *Proverbs 3:5 – Trust in the Lord with all your heart and lean not on your own understanding in All your ways acknowledge Him.*

What God has for us is never in our past. Therefore we must learn how to let it go. God has something better than that old relationship. He has something greater than your worries. He has something bigger than your fears and He has something that surpasses all pain and disappointments. God has something in your future to celebrate and it's not your past mistakes or your past misfortunes.

God wants to celebrate your future, but we must trust in Him, stand strong, and let go. One thing I've learned, you can't move forward to the new and wonderful things if you keep holding on to the past.

Think about when you drive a car. When you drive, do you spend the majority of your time looking in your rear-view mirror? The rear-view mirror represents your past. The rear-view mirror is only to be used for a short period of time. Your rear-view mirror is to remind you of where you came from, to tell you it's safe to change lanes, and it allows you to go backwards, but only for a short duration.

You can't use your rear-view mirror (your past) to move you forward to your future. If you continue to look in the rear-view mirror while trying to go forward you'll crash. But you can learn from your past and remember how God has worked in your life. Remember, how He brought you out, how He made a way out of no way, and if He did it before He can do it again. But your past is the past. Stop looking in the rear-view mirror and let it go.

The vehicle I created above, can be called the car of life. You can't drive in the car of life down the long stretch of roads without sometimes hitting a few speed bumps like regrets, disappointments, addictions, and tragedies. We all hit a few pot holes called guilt, shame, and unforgiveness. When we do, it's easy to get stuck in life's traffic jams, gaze back into our rear-view mirror and focus on our past and not remember God's promises and the future He has for us.

Looking back will distract you from what is in front of you. The devil will try to remind you of your past mistakes, your past sins, and your past failures. He will say, "You messed up, God doesn't love you." I want to say it loud and clear: *Satan is a liar.*

You are where God wants you to be. Don't dwell on the past. Keep moving forward! Let go of the wheel, get out of the driver's seat, and let God take control. He knows the detours, the traffic delays, and the construction areas. And He also knows the short cuts, and the express lanes.

Most importantly, He knows the best and safest route for you to take. What's in the rear-view mirror that keeps you holding on to your past and from moving forward?

Brothers, I do not consider myself to have taken hold of it. But one thing I do: Forgetting what is behind and reaching forward to what is ahead, I press toward the goal the prize of the upward call of God in Christ Jesus (**Philippians 3:13-14**).

God wants you to move on to the future He has planned for you. It's a future filled with hope. It's a future filled love, joy, and promises. But to get there, you must turn your focus forward and look through the windshield at the future and the road ahead.

KNOW WHO AND WHAT IS RIDING WITH YOU

Who and what are you carrying on this life's journey? The questions I would like for you to ask yourself today are, "What are you carrying that's weighing you down? What are you holding on to that's keeping you from moving forward? What moment, what issue, what person, or what event are you allowing to take space and control over your mind?"

That's the problem. We are over packed for the journey; we have too much luggage weighing us down. We continue to carry guilt, shame, hurt, pain, disappointment, wrath, jealousy, selfishness, loneliness, bitterness, low self-esteem, and in many cases, anger. Maybe I haven't looked in your suitcase, but there is something we are all carrying that the Lord has told us to let go.

We need to surround ourselves with people who support our decision to move on, to live a God-filled, purposeful life. Do your friends encourage you or discourage you? Do they push you forward, closer to your purpose and dreams or do they continually remind you of your past? Do they lift you up or tear you down?

Who's in your community? What type of accountability partners do you have? Who's in the car riding along with you? Maybe it's time for them to be let out.

My grandmother always told me to be careful of my friends. She said, "You can't soar like an eagle if you continue to hang with the chickens." Those are the doubters, the unbelievers, the naysayers, the life-suckers. Understand that God brings everyone into your life for a reason and a season. Some seasons are going to be longer than others. Ask Him to help you discern which people are to ride with you for a lifetime and which ones need to catch a Lyft or Uber.

> *Whenever you face trials of many kinds, know that the testing of your faith produces perseverance.*

Ask God for the courage and strength to keep going. He didn't bring you this far to leave you now. The Lord says be strong and of good courage, fear not, I am with you; I will strengthen you. Don't think that your best days are behind you. Expect God to continue to bless you in new ways and continue to let go and press forward.

- Let go of yesterday—trust God for tomorrow! You cannot change your past but you can change everything about your future.

- Don't dwell on the past setbacks, don't waddle in past disappointments ... release it, let it go.

- Accept what is, let go of what was, and have faith in what will be.

- Remember that your past doesn't determine your future.

- Know you can't go to your destiny if you stay in your history.

Consider it pure joy, my brothers and sisters, whenever you face trials of many kinds, because you know that the testing of your faith produces perseverance. Let perseverance finish its work so that you may be perfect and complete, lacking nothing (**James 1:2-4**).

~NOTES~

~NOTES~

CHAPTER FOUR

Hold On

*Then Jacob was left alone; and a Man wrestled with him
until the breaking of day. Now when He saw that He
did not prevail against him, He touched the socket of his
hip; and the socket of Jacob's hip was out of joint as He
wrestled with him. And He said, 'Let Me go, for the day
breaks.' But he said, 'I will not let You go unless You
bless me!'*

Genesis 32:24-26

Jacob remembered how badly he had treated his
brother, Esau, and sent word of his travel with
multiple gifts and asked for grace and forgiveness.
Jacob heard that his brother was coming to meet him
and became worried and fearful. Let me remind you,
Jacob not only tricked Esau once, but twice. First by
having Esau sell his birthright for a cup of stew and

secondly by deceiving Isaac when he dressed in an animal's skin to appear to be hairy so that Issac would bless him instead of Esau. Now let's think. If someone broke into your house and stole your stuff wouldn't you be mad? What if they didn't steal from you once but twice. It would be even worse if it were someone you knew, especially a family member. Jacob believed Esau was angry and this anger had built up for 20 years. In his mind, Esau was coming with an army of 400 men to kill him, his wives, and his children.

Jacob felt if he had acted right towards his brother in the first place then he wouldn't fear him coming. But he knew he had done wrong. There are some things that we all have done that we aren't proud of; we regret our actions and may feel like God is mad at us. Jacob prayed to God that he might be delivered from the hand of Esau. While he was praying he felt a man take hold of him. Jacob wrestled with this man all night. The man couldn't get Jacob to stop fighting or stop wrestling even though he could have easily defeated Jacob. He touched Jacob's side and his hip came out of socket. But Jacob kept fighting and fighting.

And then the angel of God said, "Let me go, for morning is coming."

Jacob replied, "I will not let you go until you bless me."

You're reading this book today because there is something you want from God. Maybe there is something you've been praying for, something you're expecting, or something you need. You want a blessing and you're wondering, *When is my time?* Jacob said, "I will not let you go until you bless me." Jacob was willing to fight for what he wanted. I'm here today to tell you God says, "Your blessing is coming, hold on." Hold on just a little while longer, your time is coming.

Have you ever felt like giving up? Have you ever felt like quitting? Have you ever felt like your situation is so hopeless that the only thing you can possibly do is leave, give up? Let's be honest, sometimes we just want to walk away, head out the door and never come back. We sometimes feel as though God has forgotten about us. At times we can feel so much emotional pain that we want to throw in the towel and say enough is enough. We say that there's no escape, no way to solve the problem, and that things are never going to get better.

Maybe God told you it was going to be all right and everything was going to be better, but you look and look for a ray of hope but all you see is darkness. God has promised you a blessing. If you just hold on a little while longer the blessing will come. But you must hold on.

I think back upon the story of Job. God took away everything he cared about, everything he had—his family, his wealth, his reputation, and his health. You can't tell me—to give up, to lose hope, to stop trusting and believing God—didn't cross his mind especially with his wife and friends in his ear. But Job kept trusting and believing in God.

Some of us fall apart when the smallest things happen; we get a flat tire, or it begins to rain, an unexpected bill shows up, and Lord have mercy if we break a fingernail. Maybe:

- You have been single for a long time and you're ready to give up on getting married or you settle for someone you know isn't right for you.

- You're the parent who is ready to give up on a disrespectful child.

- You're that pregnant teenager who can't see any way out but to have an abortion.

- You're that fed-up employee who wants to tell off the boss and walk out the door because you've been over-looked time and time again for a promotion.

- You're the victim of cancer who's tired of fighting the illness and thinking of taking your own life.

A feeling may come upon you that the situation is hopeless, that things aren't going to get better, and your prayers never will be answered. Then the spirit of temptation sneaks in ... the spirit of giving up or giving in comes in to your mind. The spirit of doing things your way, in your timing, becomes an idea. Sometimes giving up takes the form of depression, suicide, divorce, or even hurting someone else. People who give up stop working, stop fighting, stop caring, stop trusting, and most importantly, stop believing. All of us have wanted to give up at some point in time, but people who have given up have lost their faith and their hope. They no longer have dreams or desires. I want to remind you to hold on.

Jacob remembered his past and how badly he treated his brother and how he tricked his father. We might not look back at what we did, but we look at what we thought we were going to do, or what we wanted to do, or where we thought we would be right now. You know those dreams and desires to:

- Go back to school
- Get a new house
- Have a better relationship with your children
- Have children
- Start a business
- Be healthier

- Be married
- Be out of debt

There's something we have all given up on. But what about God's promises that haven't come to pass? Do you trust Him? Do you believe Him? Are you waiting patiently for it? Or have you given up on Him, too?

GOD HAS NEVER GIVEN UP ON YOU, SO WHY WOULD YOU GIVE UP ON HIM?

My question to you today is "Why do we quit?" I believe the answer encompasses various reasons, but it boils down to the lack of faith.

- Impatience – it's taking too long to come to fruition.
- Fear
- Failure
- Embarrassment
- Past
- Doubt
- Am I sure I'm the one.
- Why bother, things aren't going to change.
- Complacency – Comfortable where you are, don't want to lose what you already have.

> ## *Faith is the substance of things hoped for, the evidence of things not seen.*

Maybe we forgot ... we are fearfully and wonderfully made. And we can do all things through Christ who strengthens us. We are not giver-uppers. We are not wimps, we are not quitters, we are not dropouts, we are not failures, we are not losers. We are more than conquerors. It doesn't matter about your past. It doesn't matter about your education. It doesn't even matter about your current situation. All that matters is what God says. Our problem is we want what we want when we want it. Our timing isn't always God's timing. The main thing we must remember is God is not a man that he would lie. For if He said it, it will be done.

We must trust and believe. We need to learn to stand still and fight. But most of all we need to learn how not to give up, how to trust Him, and to hold on. Believe me, tests will come, trials will come, tribulations will come. There will be times when we're going to get tired and weak. We will get frustrated but we must hold on.

Some days, it may seem easier to give up, but Galatians 6:9 says, "So let's not get tired of doing what is good. At just the right time we will reap a harvest of blessing if we don't give up. We shall reap, if we don't lose heart, don't give up and continue to do what's right." We must have the spirit of Jacob and say, "I will not let go, I will not stop, I will not give up, I will persevere until you bless me." The Scripture tells us that if we don't give up we will see the reward.

For example, the farmer sows his seed. He takes the little seed and plants it. He does not see the grains immediately; he waits for the rain and at the proper time, a harvest. When the farmer goes and collects during the harvest season he doesn't collect what he sowed but several measures more than what he had sown. If this is true for a farmer don't you believe the same principle applies for us, too?

KEEP LOOKING FORWARD

Remember what you prayed for ... the seed you planted. The only thing is to wait patiently until we see results and hold on. 1 Corinthians 2:9 says, "But as it is written: 'Eye has not seen, nor ear heard, Nor have entered into the heart of man, The things which God has prepared for those who love Him.'" Every dream, every desire, everything you need, everything you have asked for will come to fruition. Don't lose your faith; hold on to God's Word. When you feel like giving up, remember why you held on for so long in the first place.

It's easy to look back and see what you don't have or how something didn't happen. Instead of replaying what has already happened and what you can't change, keep looking ahead. Look at what God has promised.

PERSEVERE

Perseverance is what we need when we want to quit. When the going gets tough you must get even tougher. At the right time—God's time—it will happen. You must continue to hold on, a little while longer.

You may not understand why God has you where you are or why you are going through what you're going through, but there is a PURPOSE. It's a purpose that honors God. It's a purpose that can bring you joy if you will trust in Him and follow Him.

I didn't say trust in your husband, your wife, kids, parents, your paycheck, or your pastor. Trust in God. When you are tempted to give up, remember God is in control, and He is loving, wise, and good. He has not abandoned you; He has not stopped caring about you. He has not forgotten about you.

You are where you are right now because that's where God wants you to be. Your current circumstances are part of His plan for you. This is not an accident. It's no coincidence or happenstance. It's not bad luck.

THIS IS GOD'S PLAN

Job said, "I know that you can do all things; no plan of yours can be withheld ... Surely I spoke of things I did not understand, things too wonderful for me to know." God knows. HOLD ON.

God has not forgotten about us. His promise is true. Daybreak is coming, morning is coming. Continue to speak in your spirit, *I'm not letting go until He blesses me.*

~NOTES~

_____

_____

_____

_____

_____

_____

_____

_____

_____

_____

_____

_____

_____

_____

_____

_____

_____

~NOTES~

CHAPTER FIVE

Distractions Delay Your Destiny

Now it happened as they went that He entered a certain village; and a certain woman named Martha welcomed Him into her house. And she had a sister called Mary, who also sat at Jesus' feet and heard His word. But Martha was distracted with much serving, and she approached Him and said, 'Lord, do You not care that my sister has left me to serve alone? Therefore tell her to help me.' And Jesus answered and said to her, 'Martha, Martha, you are worried and troubled about many things. But one thing is needed, and Mary has chosen that good part, which will not be taken away from her.'

Luke 10:38-42

In the above text we learn that Mary and Martha were

sisters who lived in the town of Bethany. These were

the same sisters of Lazarus that Jesus raised from the dead. Mary and Martha loved each other and shared the load of what we would call household duties — keeping the house clean and cooking.

But today, Mary heard Jesus was coming to dinner and got so excited she didn't follow her normal routine. It had been a long time since she had seen Jesus. He had been away teaching and preaching and she couldn't wait to hear His stories. Finally, Jesus and His disciples arrived, and Martha greeted them at the door. She showed them in and went back to cooking.

However, Mary sat down and began to listen to Jesus. Keep in mind this is the same woman who anointed Jesus with oil and wiped His feet with her hair. While Mary sat and listened to Jesus, Martha tried to get dinner ready. She wanted everything to be "just right" for the meal. How often do you get to serve Jesus? She wanted everything to look and taste perfectly!

But Martha got tired of doing all the work by herself, so she complained to Jesus and said, "Lord, don't you see my sister isn't helping me, it isn't fair that I am doing all the work while Martha just sits there! Tell her to come and help me."

Jesus answered, "Martha, Martha, [you know with that shaking of the head tone] you worry about too many things. What Mary is hearing is more important to her than serving or eating. She has chosen the right thing for her and it will not be taken away."

Wow! Jesus spoke up for Mary, even though Martha thought she was being lazy. Mary knew what was important for her, spending time with Jesus and listening to His teaching! Many of us make the same mistake Martha made. We get so busy worried about what other people are or aren't doing. We are not focused on what God has called us to do. We get distracted by the daily activities of the world: going to work, school, church, sporting events, community events, going, going, going, that we often forget the most important thing—what does God want us to do? We forget to spend time with Him! We must be careful that we don't get so busy doing things we think are good, that we leave out the best thing, Jesus!

In this story with Martha and Mary, Martha was focused with serving, not a bad thing. For the Bible says we are to serve one another humbly in love. Yet, she was distracted by focusing on what Mary was (or was not depending on how you look at it) doing. Our lives are full of distractions. Distractions get in our way of making God's purpose and plan the number one priority in our life. Many of us are busy but we aren't doing anything. We must follow God's purpose and plan for our life, like Mary, and not focus on what others may want us to do.

> *Many are the plans in a person's heart, but it is the LORD's purpose that prevails.*
> **Proverbs 19:21**

What is distracting you from God's purpose? What's holding you back from your breakthrough? What's holding you back from your victory? What's keeping you from your promises? What's holding up your blessing?

God's made us some promises. He said we are the head and not the tail. He said we are more than conquerors. Do you believe His Word? And we know that His Word shall not return to Him void. Still we wonder, *where are the promises? When is my time?* Perhaps you've been praying, fasting, and serving but you haven't received that promise. You haven't been healed, you haven't received the promotion, you haven't gotten married, you weren't approved for the new house. Remove the distractions. Distractions delay your destiny.

God's purpose, promise, and plan for our lives was established before we were created. Before we were formed in the womb He knew us. Before we were born He sanctified us. He ordained us for such a time as this.

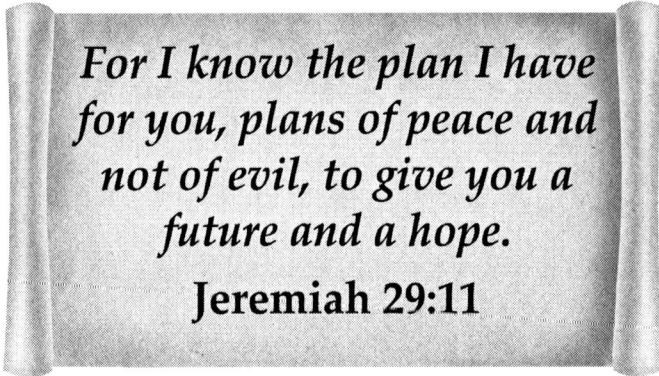

> **For I know the plan I have for you, plans of peace and not of evil, to give you a future and a hope.**
> **Jeremiah 29:11**

But to know God's plan, to walk in His purpose, to receive His promise, we must be in Divine Alignment with Him. That means we must remove some distractions—the confusion, the clutter, the junk, the stuff that not only enters our lives but enter our minds.

We all have distractions, but what are we doing to remove them? In order to remove a distraction we must first know what a distraction is.

DISTRACTION - DISTRACTION - DISTRACTION

In its Latin origin, distraction is "distrahere," which means pulling apart, or separation. It is defined as: 1) something that prevents someone from giving their full attention to something else, 2) something that makes it difficult to think or pay attention, 3) agitation of the mind or emotions.

Distractions mess with our minds and our feelings. The law of physics says two things can't occupy the same space. Therefore, if something is already in your head or if something is already talking to you and has your attention, it's harder for you to hear from God. He who has ears to hear, let him hear! My questions to you are, "What and who are you listening to? What has you attention?"

Distractions can be many things. It can be something as simple as the phone ringing, or people talking to you when you are trying to focus on something else or pulling you away from something, or maybe even the TV shows you watch. But what if your distraction is something that's not obvious? Maybe it's the people you hang with, or even the food you eat. Maybe it's holding on to hurt, or not being happy about who you are.

Social media and reality TV shows have become a huge distraction. If you are focused on what someone else is doing, what they have posted, how many likes or views they (or you) have, you can't focus on what God is trying to tell you or show you. We need to stop focusing so much on television and get off of Snapchat,

Instagram, Facebook and get with the Lord and get in "The Book." I know it's easy to say, but hard for us to do. Many people are addicted to social media and television and will spend hours following what other people are saying and doing.

The enemy comes to steal, kill, and destroy. It is not a secret, the enemy will tempt us by distracting us with things we like. He's not going to distract us with something we don't like. He knows what we like. He knows our weaknesses and that's where he will attack the hardest, although most likely, in a concealed way.

We must be led by the spirit of God and be in alignment with His plan and His timing. We can't say Lord, here I am, tell me what you want, I'll do whatever you ask me to do, *but* … . What is your but? What is the thing you won't let go? What is your distraction? Is it smoking, cursing, fornicating, lying, or gluttony? Maybe it's a relationship or a TV show. Perhaps it's not even one show but the amount of TV you're watching. What area of your life is missing the mark? Any act or thought that falls short of God's will is a sin. Sin is sin and sin is a distraction. What is your distraction?

There are some things God has told you let go of, but you love them too much. It's easy to let go of those things we don't like. But what about the things you like but aren't good for you?

Do not love the world or the things in the world. If anyone loves the world, the love of the Father is not in him. For all that is in the world—the lust of the flesh, the lust of the eyes, and the pride of life—is not of the Father but is of the world. And the world is passing away, and the lust of it; be he who does the will of God abides forever (**1 John 2:15-17**).

Ephesians 6:12 states, "For we do not wrestle against flesh and blood, but against principalities, against powers, against the rulers of the darkness of this age, against spiritual hosts of wickedness in the heavenly places. "

Do not love the world or the things in the world. If anyone loves the world, the love of the Father is not in him.

1 John 2:15

To all of my single Christians, don't get discouraged, don't get upset, and don't get angry while you're in the season of singleness. God has you exactly where He wants you to be. 1 Corinthians 7:32-35 states, "But I want you to be without care. He who is unmarried cares for the things of the Lord—how he may please the Lord. But he who is married cares about the things of the world—how he may please his wife. The unmarried woman cares about the things of the Lord, that she may be holy both in body and in spirit. But she who is married cares about the things of the world—how she may please her husband. And this I say for your own profit, that you may serve the Lord without distraction."

Many single people focus so much on getting married, that they forget to focus on what God wants them to do right now. The Word says it is good for the unmarried to stay unmarried so they can focus on the Lord. But IF they cannot control themselves, let them marry. If you are focused on doing the will of God you won't be so easily distracted by the fleshly desires of man.

I remember my Bishop asking me one day, "Are you single because you're busy or are you busy because you're single?"

My answer was then and still is "Yes!"

Don't get me wrong, I have a desire to be married, however in this season while God is preparing me for my spouse, I will continue to grow and do His will. I realize our number one distraction is us. It isn't the enemy but the "inner me." It's in our head. It's the self-doubt, the low self-esteem and the lack of faith.

For as he thinks in his heart, so is he (**Proverbs 23:7**).

Once again, we must let go of our past. The enemy will come and try to fill us with doubt and disbelief to convince us that God doesn't love us, and that God doesn't care. He wants us to believe we are all alone. But know God will never leave us nor forsake us. What past guilt, shame, hurt, pain, regrets, disappointments, and tragedies are distracting you from your future?

If we claim to be without sin, we deceive ourselves and the truth is not in us. But God has forgiven us and has forgotten about our past mistakes, ~~our past issues,~~ and our past indiscretions. Why do some people keep beating up on themselves and re-living their past over and over again in their mind? We MUST set our minds on things above. We cannot set them on earthly things and the past.

Lastly, the devil will try to distract you when you're weak, tired, in pain and hurting, both physically and emotionally. That's why it's important to stay prayed up and to get proper rest and eat the right foods. When you're in pain, he'll try to lure you with quick fixes; drugs, alcohol, a non-attachable partner encounter. He wants you to believe the distraction will fix all of your problems. But those are only distractions. Distractions delay your destiny.

This is the time you must seek God. Don't get tired, don't get weary, don't run to the bottle, or another person. Stay strong and recognize it for what it is, a distraction.

Mary knew what was important to her ... spending time with Jesus. She didn't let Martha distract her from her purpose. Stay focused on what God has called YOU to do.

Seek first the kingdom of God and His righteousness, and all these things shall be added to you (**Matthew 6:33**).

Delay is not denial. Keep the faith, stay focused, keep pressing, and move the distractions out of the way.

~NOTES~

~NOTES~

CHAPTER SIX

Beware of the Counterfeits

Then if anyone says to you, 'Look, here is the Christ!'
or 'There!' do not believe it. For false christs and false
prophets will rise and show great signs and wonders to
deceive, if possible, even the elect. See, I have told you
beforehand. 'Therefore if they say to you, 'Look, He is in
the desert!' do not go out; or 'Look, He is in the inner
rooms!' do not believe it. For as the lightning comes from
the east and flashes to the west, so also will the coming of
the Son of Man be. For wherever the carcass is, there the
eagles will be gathered together.

Matthew 24:23-28

Just like distractions, counterfeits will arise in your
life to take you away from your purpose, your will,
and your destiny. What is a counterfeit?

Counterfeit—something or someone, made in exact imitation of something valuable or important, with the intention to deceive or defraud you. Counterfeits may come close to the real thing. You may actually feel it is the real thing but it's not. It's an imitation. It's a fake.

Single people look for a perfect mate and all of us believe … This is the one. Everything may look good on the outside … polite, attractive, good job, makes great money, and may even attend church. But something doesn't seem right. It looks real, but is it? Is it authentic?

Trust and believe, when you are waiting on "the one" God has just for you, and you're walking in His purpose, in obedience and faith, the enemy will send someone or something to run interference, to get you out of God's will, to get you off of course. The enemy's plan is to steal, kill, and destroy you. The easiest way to do this is to lure you away from what God has for you.

Has God ordained this relationship or situation? Counterfeits are not only found in relationships, but they come to invade job offers, business endeavors, and every area in our life to keep us from God's full purpose.

When you seek God's wisdom and ask for the spirit of discernment, He will reveal to you the counterfeits in your life as quickly as a Pucci (Gucci) or a knock off

Louis Vuitton or Hermes on one of the street corners of New York City's Time Square. Edgar Allan Poe once said, "Believe nothing you hear, and only half that you see." I would say, believe nothing you hear and nothing you see with your physical eye. We must know the spirit by the spirit.

Do not believe every spirit, but test the spirits, whether they are of God; because many false prophets have gone out into the world. By this you know the Spirit of God (**1 John 4:1**).

Not only do we need to recognize the counterfeits, we must not accept the counterfeits in our life. A counterfeit relationship, job, or situation, is just like a counterfeit pocketbook. They don't last that long. They begin to look worn, frazzled, and abused. Most of all, they have little or no value. Too many times we settle for less than God wants us to have because we are tired of waiting.

Wait on the Lord, And keep His way, And He shall exalt you to inherit the land (**Psalm 37:34**).

Don't settle for a fraction of what you're worth. Don't think you have to settle for less, be less, or have less than your dreams, desires, and especially God's promises. I once heard someone say, "You can't claim the gold, if you settle for bronze." Decide that you will not accept a counterfeit. Decide that you want the real authentic promise and know you are worth it. God wants you to have life and have it more abundantly. Don't settle for crumbs when a seven-course meal is set before you.

Make up in your mind that everything you've been through is preparing you for your promises.

NEVER ACCEPT LESS THAN GOD'S BEST!

Don't settle for what you see, don't settle for what you know, and don't settle for what you are comfortable with. Continue to press towards your dreams and your promises beyond your comfort zone.

~NOTES~

_____

_____

_____

_____

_____

_____

_____

_____

_____

_____

_____

_____

_____

_____

_____

_____

_____

_____

_____

~NOTES~

CHAPTER SEVEN

Come out of Your Comfort Zone

Now the Lord had said to Abram: 'Get out of your country, From your family And from your father's house, To a land that I will show you. I will make you a great nation; I will bless you And make your name great; And you shall be a blessing. I will bless those who bless you, And I will curse him who curses you; And in you all the families of the earth shall be blessed.'

Genesis 12:1-4

Abram was called to leave his country, family, and everything familiar to go to a place he did not even know about. God didn't said leave and go to Atlanta, Charlotte, Houston, or Chicago. He didn't even say Japan or London. He said get out and I will show you.

During this time, only landless, homeless, or fugitives moved about and left their people. Abram wasn't a young man, he was 75 years old and he was the next in line of authority. Let's put this story in perspective and be honest. It's hard to uproot, change, and leave what you're accustomed to even when you know where you're going and why you're going.

In today's terms, Abram had a beautiful wife, was married for 50 plus years, had acres and acres of land and cattle, worked for the same company for over 60 years and was about to be promoted to CEO. He didn't have any property taxes, light bill, or gas bill to pay. Everything was taken care of. And God told him, "Okay. It's time for you to leave from what's familiar to you. You've got to go!"

Many of us would have said, "God is that truly you? I need a sign." But Abram was faithful and obedient. He left as instructed and stepped outside his comfort zone. And because of his obedience he was blessed.

Many of us have comfort zones. It may be our jobs, our homes, the color of our hair or the way we wear our hair, the style of our clothes, the friends we have, the same route we take to the grocery store or to work every day, even the seat we sit in at church or a meeting. What is your comfort zone? Comfort zone —a place or situation where you feel safe, comfortable, at ease, where you don't have to take risk. In your comfort zone, there is no growth and where there isn't any growth, there isn't any progress. Growth only occurs when we take risk, when we try something new and step out of your comfort zone in obedience to God.

God asked Abram to leave his comfort zone. Abraham had to leave everything he knew (his family, his friends, his country, his home) in order to follow God. The trip wasn't a short trip. It took months, and it was full of what we would consider unwelcome circumstances. This wasn't an easy journey. Abram faced obstacles—animals, thieves, and fatigue. But Abram could not experience God's blessing if he stayed inside his comfort zone in his home in Haran. To experience God's blessing, we must come out of our comfort zone.

For all my sports fans—a common terminology often used is—he's in the zone or she's in the zone. Being "in the zone" is usually a good thing. In baseball, get it in the strike zone. In football, get in the red zone to score a touchdown. Anyone who has known me even for a little while knows I love sports and because of my regulatory professional job, I'm all about following the rules, but for a minute indulge me. Suppose God wants to use you—"outside the zone?"

What if He is calling you to do something that feels uncomfortable and not natural? In other words, you don't have that McDonald's "I'm loving it" feeling. What if it means you must step outside your comfort zone and let God work through you? What if it means doing something totally out of your nature and character? What if it means people may think you are crazy?

Getting out of your comfort zone may feel like punishment. You may ask God, "Isn't there an easier way than me speaking in public? Do I have to start a new job? Do I have to move to a new city? Do I have to break up with this boyfriend or girlfriend? Do I have to go back to school? Can't someone else do it? Better yet, no one else has done it that way, why me?"

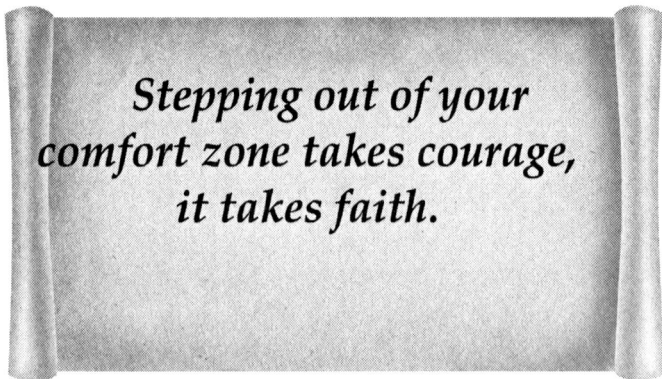

> *Stepping out of your comfort zone takes courage, it takes faith.*

What have you hoped for, what have you prayed for, what has God shown you in the spirit but you're afraid to go after it? Abram was called by God to go to a place he had never seen, a place where he was to receive his inheritance without knowing where he was going. The question is, can you follow God and get out of your comfort zone but yet remain comfortable in God's arms when you don't know what's next?

There are three things I noticed that we do to get out of our comfort zone. One, we are people-pleasers. Instead of pleasing God we have gotten into the people pleasing business. Don't say that's not you. There are few people who truly don't care what other people think about them. However, being a people-pleaser will affect your relationship with God. Being a people-pleaser will affect your ability to make good decisions. Being a people-pleaser will also wear you out. Why do we want to please people? We learn as small children that pleasing others brings rewards. *If I finish all my food I'll get dessert. If I finish my homework I can go play. If I get good grades and keep my room clean, I'll get a new toy.*

Unfortunately, in many areas of our lives, that mentality carried over from our childhood to our work. *If I stay late and finish a report on time, the boss will remember me during promotion time.* We even do it in our relationships. *I wonder if he likes this dress. I hope she likes this cologne.* Our actions have geared us to pleasing others instead of pleasing God. When was the last time you did something and didn't care what anyone else thought, but only how God felt? Pleasing those we love is rewarding, and there is nothing wrong with that.

However, we can't let our desire to please people and gain their approval become as important or more as pleasing God. Pleasing God is a higher calling and much more fulfilling. Whatever you do in word or deed should be done in the name of Jesus, giving glory to God, not to please man.

People-pleasers also live in fear that others will learn of their past failures, their mistakes, and their shortcomings. This brings me to the second point to get out of our comfort zone—quit explaining yourself. People try to remind you about your past, your past failures, your past mistakes, your past hiccups. Stop trying to justify or explain what you did, where you've been, or what you're going through. Everyone has a "past" and we all have made mistakes. The Bible reminds us in Romans 3:23 that we all have sinned and fallen short of His glory. We must remember God is bigger than our past. And when people bring up your mishaps your answer should be—"So what? We live and we learn." We must make sure we learn from our mistakes. Every mistake brings growth if you allow it. Your mistakes build up your prayer life.

"Brothers and sisters, I know that I still have a long way to go. But there is one thing I do: I forget what is in the past and try as hard as I can to reach the goal before me" (Philippians 3:13).

Stop bringing up your past. God has forgotten about it, so why haven't you? Your past experiences are not weights or stumbling blocks. They are stairs. They're stepping stones to help you to rise up to the next level.

Don't remember the prior things; or consider the things of old. Look! I'm doing a new thing; now it sprouts up; don't you recognize it? I'm making a way in the desert, paths in the wilderness (**Isaiah 43:18-1**9).

So you tried something new and it didn't work out, don't give up, but instead learn from it and keep it moving. Proverbs 24:16 states, "For the righteous falls seven times and rises again, but the wicked stumble in times of calamity" (Proverbs 24:16).

God can do extraordinary things with ordinary people, but we must be willing to step out of our comfort zone. Maybe that means leaving your job or asking that person out you were scared to approach. It could mean going back to school, buying a new car, starting you own business, writing a book, speaking in public, or singing in the choir. What is God telling you to do that is outside of your comfort zone? It may not be easy at first, but it's only in the uncomfortable place that we rely on Him. You keep wondering, *when is my time?* Have you ever thought God may be waiting for you to step out of your comfort zone? Staying in your comfort zone hinders you from your future, your success, your blessing, and your greatness. Instead, you settle for mediocre.

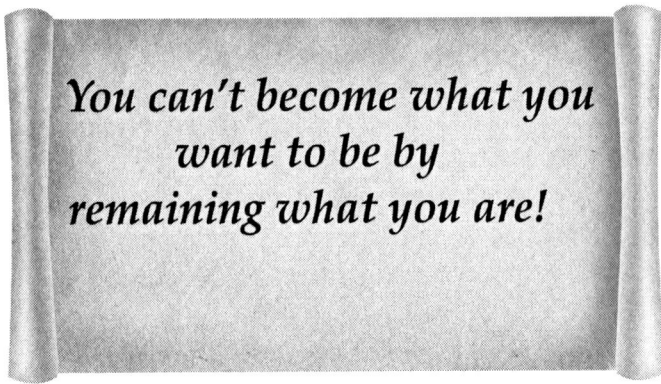

> **You can't become what you want to be by remaining what you are!**

If you want to break free from your comfort zone you may need to break free from some of the people you hang around. The way you act, the way you speak, the way you think is directly affected by your friends. Birds of a feather flock together. If they are comfortable in their current situation why would they want you to move? We read in 1 Corinthians 15:33, "Do not be deceived 'Evil company corrupts good habits.'"

Do your friends encourage you or discourage you? Do they lift you up or tear you down? Who's on your team? Do they push you closer to your dreams, your future, and your desires or do they laugh at your aspirations, tear you down and hold you back? In football, holding is a penalty. In basketball holding is a foul and if you get too many you get thrown out the game. Some people have been holding you back too long and it's time for you to throw a flag, give them a technical and throw them out of the game of your life and your future.

STEPPING OUT OF YOUR COMFORT ZONE MEANS TO WALK IN FAITH

It's time for you to move to where God wants you to be. 1 Peter 2:9 states, "Called you out of darkness into the marvelous light." Some of us would rather sit in the dark. God is trying to give us the world but we won't even leave our front porch. We grow only by leaving our comfort zone. We rely on God and we become spiritually larger.

I'm not telling you to change who you are, just stretch the box you're in to reach the full potential God has for you. Stepping out of your comfort zone might be uncomfortable, awkward, embarrassing, and fearful. But you must continue to walk with boldness in the face of uncertainty and trust in God's Word.

Let me remind you of the Israelites. They wandered in the wilderness for 40 years. They wanted to go back to Egypt, to their comfort zone, to what they were used to. But they had to trust God. God will call every one of us out of our comfort zone at one point in time or another. God wants to push us into our destiny. The question is, "Will you follow His command and be obedient?" God knows you. He knows every hair on your head and knows exactly what you can do. He has equipped you with everything you need for this next stage of your life. All you must do is trust and believe Him and come out of your comfort zone.

When is my time? Hold on to your God-given promises. Know that you are planted here on earth with a God-given purpose that only you were created to manifest. Continue to please God in word and deed, knowing that trials and tribulations will come to tempt you and distract you. Beware of the things that are not of God but allow Him to use you in an extraordinary, unusual only "God can do" way. As long as you continue to hold on to His Word, and never let go of your faith you will overcome and see, your time is now.

But as for me, I trust in You, O Lord; I say, 'You are my God.' My times are in Your hand (**Psalm 31:14-15**).

~NOTES~

~NOTES~

Acknowledgments

I give glory and honor to my Heavenly Father for the inspiration and motivation to write this book. I thank each of you for taking the time to read what God gave me and pray that it provided encouragement and uplifted you.

I thank Tyrone Ashley for the design of the clock, used throughout the book.

To Karen and Rodney Way, I couldn't ask for a better support team. Thanks for always being there. Your words of encouragement and your actions of love cannot be measured.

Special thanks to Bishop Fuller, my spiritual father, pastor, and friend, for always pushing me, stretching me to new heights and not allowing me to say no. Thanks, for seeing in me what I sometimes don't see in myself.

In addition, I want to thank everyone who knowingly and unknowingly played a part in helping me along this journey.

To God be the glory!

ABOUT THE AUTHOR

Rev Tamara Elcan Baldwin is a native of Chicago, Illinois and attended Christ Universal Temple as a child into her teenage years where she was very active in many ministries.

She currently resides outside of Augusta, GA where she is an associate minister at Macedonia Church of Augusta under the leadership of Bishop Gregory Fuller. While at Macedonia she has been active with several ministries to include: Youth & Children's Church Director, Worship & Arts Ministry, Single's Ministry Coordinator, and the Women of Virtue Ministry.

Rev. Baldwin attended Tuskegee University where she earned a Bachelor's of Science in Chemical Engineering and Chemistry. She also earned a Masters of Engineering and Technology Management degree and is currently pursuing a Masters in Divinity.

Rev. Baldwin's love for God, love for children, and love for people in general has afforded her the opportunity to minister across the world and receive numerous awards for community service, empowerment, and academic excellence. Outside of church she continues to work with other organizations, including her sorority, Delta Sigma Theta Sorority, Inc., to empower others and spreading the word of God.

Her Favorite Scripture: Colossians 3:17 - And whatever you do, whether in word or deed, do it all in the name of the Lord Jesus, giving thanks to God the Father through him.